by Fern Nichols
Founder
Moms in Prayer International

All you need to know to start or join a group!

Scripture quotations taken from the New American Standard Bible® (NASB), Copyright © 1960, 1962, 1963, 1968, 1971, 1972, 1973, 1975, 1977, 1995 by The Lockman Foundation Used by permission. www.Lockman.org

Scripture quotations taken from the Amplified® Bible (AMP), Copyright © 2015 by The Lockman Foundation, La Habra, CA 90631. All rights reserved. Used by permission. www.Lockman.org

Scripture quotations are taken from the Holy Bible, New Living Translation, Copyright ©1996, 2004, 2007, 2013, 2015 by Tyndale House Foundation. Used by permission of Tyndale House Publishers, Inc., Carol Stream, IL 60188. All rights reserved.

Scripture taken from the New King James Version®. Copyright © 1982 by Thomas Nelson, Inc. Used by permission. All rights reserved.

ESV Copyright and Permissions Information The Holy Bible, English Standard Version® (ESV®) Copyright © 2001 by Crossway, a publishing ministry of Good News Publishers. All rights reserved.

Scripture references marked (KJV): Public Domain

Corroborating resource: BibleGateway.com

Notice

No portion of this publication may be translated into any language or reproduced in any form, except for brief quotations, without prior written permission of the author.

Copyright © 1987 Fern Nichols. All rights reserved.
First to sixteenth printings, 1987-2009.
Seventeenth printing, September 2012 revised from
Moms In Touch International to Moms in Prayer International.
Twenty-First printing, August 2020.
Printed in the United States of America.
ISBN 978-1-929477-52-4

Moms in Prayer International
P.O. Box 1120, Poway, California 92074-1120, USA

Phone: 858.486.2528
Email: info@MomsInPrayer.org
MomsInPrayer.org

Table of Contents

Introduction 4
Fern's Testimony 6
Mission and Vision Statements 8
Purpose 8
What is Moms in Prayer? 9
Start a Group / Join a Group 9
Helpful Suggestions for Your Prayer Group 10
Praying in One Accord 11
Prayer Time: *Four Steps of Prayer* 12
    ❧ Praise 12
    ❧ Confession 13
    ❧ Thanksgiving 14
    ❧ Intercession 15
Prayer Suggestions for Our Children 16
Prayer Suggestions for Teachers & Staff 17
Prayer Suggestions for Schools 18
Prayer Suggestions for Moms in Prayer International 19
Prayer Sheet Information 19
Praying for the Non-believer 20
Promises to Claim 21
Words and Deeds 23
Statement of Faith 24
Policies 26
Core Values and Guiding Principles 28
Find a Group / Start a Group 29
Frequently Asked Questions 30
Supporting the Ministry 31
Registration Info 32
Prayer Sheet .... Center Insert

Introduction

My heart was heavy as I sent my two eldest children to their first day of public junior high school. That fall day in 1984, I was burdened with concern for the new world they were entering. I knew they would face their greatest test in resisting immoral values, vulgar language and peer pressure. My heart cried out to the Lord asking Him to protect them, to enable them to see clearly the difference between right and wrong, and to guide them in making good decisions.

The burden to intercede for my boys was so overwhelming that I knew I could not bear it alone. I asked God to give me another mom who felt the same burden and who would be willing to pray with me concerning our children and their school. God heard the cry of my heart and led me to phone another mom who voiced her agreement as I shared my burden. We also thought of a few other moms who might want to pray with us. We called them and began meeting for prayer the following week.

This was the beginning of the interdenominational, Christian prayer movement Moms in Prayer International (formerly known as Moms In Touch). As moms began sharing what God had been doing in their lives, and in the lives of their children because of prayer, other groups began to spring up all over British Columbia where we were living at the time. Groups formed for elementary through high school levels. The initial material in this *Booklet* was formulated during that year. What a thrill to see God's plan unfold!

The summer of 1985 brought a change to our family as we moved from Abbotsford, British Columbia, to Poway, California. I soon discovered that God was giving me still greater opportunities for carrying on the work that began in Canada. I prayed God would raise up moms who were willing to intercede for their children.

God has been faithful to send us women who will pray. Moms in Prayer groups now meet in every state in the USA and in more than 140 other countries. Because moms were asking how to pray and how to begin a Moms in Prayer group, we created this *Booklet*.

I would like to acknowledge Sondra Ball, who helped me compile this material. Her encouragement, suggestions, time, friendship and loving support have been specific answers to my prayers.

I pray that God will raise up moms to intercede for every school in our nation and around the world. What a thrilling thought to consider two or more moms gathered together every week in prayer for their children and their schools.

Let me challenge you to be involved in your child's life through prayer. See what God can do for your children and their schools when you are faithful to pray with at least one other mom on a regular basis.

Believing in the power of God through prayer,

Fern Nichols

Fern Nichols

> *Arise, cry out in the night,*
> *at the beginning of the night watches!*
> *Pour out your heart like water before the presence of the Lord!*
> *Lift your hands to him for the lives of your children,*
> *who faint for hunger at the head of every street.*
>
> Lamentations 2:19 (ESV)

Fern's Testimony

I would like to share how God has worked in my personal life regarding prayer. Many years ago, I was asked to speak at a prayer retreat which resulted in a serious evaluation of my prayer life. Listening to several tapes on prayer by Ron Dunn helped me greatly. I also read wonderful books on prayer, but I knew within my heart that listening to discussions about prayer, talking about prayer, or reading about prayer didn't make up for my lack of actually praying.

I seemed to always be praying "on the run." My prayer time was hit and miss. God, in His grace, allowed me to see that my priorities were not right. I was busy being productive in many wonderful things, but I wasn't doing the best thing—spending consistent prayer time with my Heavenly Father.

I believe Satan has us thinking that being spiritual means being productive. He doesn't want us to cross over the invisible line into powerful, intercessory prayer. If he can keep us thinking that being on the productive side of the line is doing great things for God, then we will secure few blessings for our family, schools, community and nation. But if we recognize the line and cross over it to be intercessors, God will move heaven and earth to answer our prayers, and we will begin to see great victories and Satan's defeat. Satan trembles when he sees the weakest saint on her knees, for he knows he has no power against our prayers that are prayed according to God's will.

Here is a list of what I asked God to do in my life in this matter of prayer.

- That I would be a woman of prayer
- That I would gain a vision for the power of God through prayer
- That I would seek to become an intercessor
- That I would begin to practice proactive praying, taking the initiative to pray with others as a way of life
- That I would learn to pray using the Scriptures
- That I would pray without ceasing
- That I would be able to communicate to others what God is teaching me in prayer

If the Holy Spirit is speaking to your heart as you read this list, stop right now, heed His voice and pray.

I believe the ministry of prayer is the highest calling a Christian can have. Right now, Jesus is seated at the right hand of God interceding for you (Romans 8:34).

> *I believe the ministry of prayer is the highest calling a Christian can have.*
>
> —Fern Nichols

Mission Statement

Moms in Prayer International impacts children and schools worldwide for Christ by gathering mothers to pray.

Vision Statement

Our vision is that every school in the world would be covered with prayer.

Purpose

- To stand in the gap for our children through prayer

- To pray that our children will receive Jesus as Lord and Savior, then stand boldly in their faith

- To pray for teachers and staff

- To pray that teachers, administrators, staff and students will come to faith in Jesus Christ

- To pray that our schools will be directed by biblical values and high moral standards

- To be an encouragement and a positive support to our schools

- To provide hope and strength to moms who carry heavy burdens for their children

What is Moms in Prayer?

Two or more women who meet regularly (one hour a week is optimal) to intercede on behalf of children and schools through prayer

Christian mothers, grandmothers or any woman who is willing to pray for a specific child and school

Women who believe that God answers prayer!

Join a Group / Start a Group

We have groups for every woman, let us help you connect. For more information on how to join or start a group contact MomsInPrayer.org to find your community. Here are some steps to take:

- Pray that God brings you another mom willing to meet with you each week for prayer.

- Read and agree with the Moms in Prayer Statement of Faith on pages 24 and 25 of this *Booklet*.

- Use the Moms in Prayer Four Steps of Prayer (see Page 12).

- Abide by the Policies and Core Values of the ministry (on Pages 28 & 29).

- Make a list of prospective moms from your school and ask them to join your prayer time.

- Visit MomsInPrayer.org to register your group or fill out and return the registration form at the back of this *Booklet*. This will enable us to refer interested moms to your group or help you find a local group to join, as well as send news and updates from the ministry.

- Encourage each group member to register online or mail in the tear-off registration form found on the last page of this *Moms in Prayer Booklet*.

- Trust God for answers to your prayer, focus on Him and expect great things to happen.

Helpful Suggestions for Your Group

As you begin:

- Come as you are.
- Be faithful in meeting for one hour on a regular basis (weekly is optimal). Stress the importance of faithful commitment to the group. Regular attendance develops consistent prayer coverage, builds trust, instills unity and strengthens the group.
- Start and finish on time.
- Read the *Moms in Prayer Booklet* periodically.
- Avoid distractions by not serving refreshments.
- Place a "Please Do Not Disturb" note on the door and silence phones.

Each mom needs:

- A Bible
- Her own *Moms in Prayer Booklet*
- Someone to care for her children if they are not in school during this hour

In matters of prayer:

- Pray conversationally in One Accord using the Four Steps of Prayer.
- Do not get sidetracked in talking about your requests. Pray about them. Share your thanksgivings and requests in prayer rather than discussing them first.
- **Keep everything that is said or prayed in a Moms in Prayer meeting confidential.** Nothing said should ever be shared with anyone outside of that group. Confidentiality cannot be overemphasized.

Praying in One Accord
Method of Prayer

Conversationally praying in one accord is the method of prayer that is used in our Moms in Prayer groups. One accord prayer is agreeing together as directed and energized by the Holy Spirit, as found in Phil 2:2 (ESV) ... *complete my joy by being of the same mind, having the same love, being in full accord and of one mind.* When a group prays in one accord, they concentrate on **one subject at a time**. More than one mom can pray on each subject until that subject is covered.

Do not be concerned about silence; God also speaks during these times. Try to keep prayers **short** and **simple**. This will encourage everyone to participate.

In her book *What Happens When Women Pray*, Evelyn Christenson says, "When people start praying together in one accord, to our Father in heaven, in the name of Jesus, and practice praying together, things begin to change. Our lives change, our families change, our school, church and communities change. Changes take place not when we study about prayer, not when we talk about it, not even when we memorize beautiful Scripture verses on prayer. It is when we actually pray that things begin to happen."

If you have never prayed conversationally before, please do not feel you must pray aloud. You may pray silently. The more you experience conversational prayer, the easier it will be for you to eventually join in.

By praying in one accord, we hear the heartfelt thoughts of others, and echo those words in our hearts as well. This will cause us to focus on Almighty God and not on ourselves. He will give you the words to say. The eloquence of your prayer is not what is important. **The sincerity of your heart is what God hears.**

All these with one accord were devoting themselves to prayer ...
Acts 1:14 a ESV

Prayer Time
Using the Four Steps of Prayer
The Moms in Prayer hour is divided into Four Steps of Prayer: Praise, Confession, Thanksgiving and Intercession.

To ensure plenty of time to thoroughly pray for your children, school and staff, we estimate about 25 minutes for Praise, Confession and Thanksgiving, and about 35 minutes devoted to Intercession.

Prayer Sheets and resources for your prayer hour are available on our website: MomsInPrayer.org

Praise—Every prayer time begins with praising God for His characteristics using His Word. Our faith becomes strong as we pray back to God what He says about Himself, praising Him for who He is and not for what He has done—no answers to prayer or requests during this time. This is God's time.

The following illustrates the method of praising God in one accord. A leader chooses an attribute (a characteristic) of God, for example, Shepherd. Select verses that reflect the attribute, such as Psalm 23:1 and Isaiah 40:11. Read them aloud. Psalm 23:1 (NASB), *The Lord is my shepherd, I shall not want.* Then read Isaiah 40:11 (NLT), *He will feed his flock like a shepherd. He will carry the lambs in his arms, holding them close to his heart. He will gently lead the mother sheep with their young.*

After reading the verses aloud, the group leader begins by praying, "Father, I praise You that You are a God who meets every need of Your children, like a shepherd providing for his sheep."

Another mom might continue by praying, "I agree, Lord. I rejoice that You care for us so deeply. Just as a shepherd knows his sheep, You know our needs."

A third mom might pray, "We praise You for giving us this beautiful picture of Yourself as our Shepherd, One who understands us and carries us in Your arms, holding us close to Your heart."

Praising God as the Shepherd continues until the subject is covered.

As we praise God:

- ❧ It exalts God and gives Him glory.
- ❧ It is declaring, proclaiming, confessing who God is.
- ❧ It is for our good. It brings freedom and encouragement to our lives because we focus on God and not our situation.
- ❧ It brings about an awareness of His Presence (Psalm 22:3).
- ❧ It dispels the enemy's power, and he is defeated. From 2 Chronicles 20:22 (NKJV), *Now when they began to sing and to praise ... [the enemy was] defeated.*

Additional Attributes of God

Faithful—Deuteronomy 7:9; Psalm 145:13; 2 Timothy 2:13

Wise—Isaiah 55:8-9; Daniel 2:20-22; Romans 11:33-34

Eternal—Psalm 90:2; Daniel 7:14; Revelation 1:8, 18

Compassionate—Psalm 103:13-14; Isaiah 30:18-19; Matthew 9:36

Holy—Exodus 15:11; Isaiah 57:15; Revelation 15:4

Creator—Jeremiah 10:12; Psalm 95:3-6; Colossians 1:16

More Attributes of God can be found in the *Leader's Guide: Leading with Strength & Grace*.

Confession—Following your time of praise, God may reveal some areas of your life that are not pleasing to Him.

The group leader invites each member to take a few moments to silently confess those sins to God. Isaiah 59:2 (AMP) tells us, *But your wickedness has separated you from your God, And your sins have hidden His face from you so that He does not hear.* God says that He will not answer our prayer if there is unconfessed sin. Our relationship must not only be right with Him, but also with others, if we desire God to hear and answer our prayers.

How do we confess our sin when convicted by the Holy Spirit?

1. Name the sin specifically, agreeing with God that it is sin.
2. Repent concerning the sin. This will result in changed attitudes and actions.

3. Thank God that He has forgiven your sin because of what Christ did on the cross. 1 John 1:9 (KJV), *If we confess our sins, he is faithful and just to forgive us our sins, and to cleanse us from all unrighteousness.*

4. Ask to be filled and controlled by the Holy Spirit. Surrender your will and make a total commitment of yourself to God.

    ᷾ **Command**—Ephesians 5:18b (NASB), *Be filled with the Spirit.*

    ᷾ **Promise**—1 John 5:14-15 (NASB), *This is the confidence which we have before Him, that, if we ask anything according to His will, He hears us. And if we know that He hears us in whatever we ask, we know that we have the requests which we have asked from Him.*

5. By faith, thank Him that He has filled you on the basis of His promise. Do not depend on your feelings. The promise of God's Word, not our feelings, is our authority.

Thanksgiving—During this time, we offer prayers of thanksgiving, expressing appreciation and gratefulness for God's answers to our prayers. In 1 Thessalonians 5:18 (KJV), the Apostle Paul exhorts, *In everything give thanks: for this is the will of God in Christ Jesus concerning you.* In Psalm 50:23a (NASB), God's Word tells us that when we give thanks we honor Him: *He who offers a sacrifice of thanksgiving honors Me.*

Instead of spending time telling the answer to your prayer, pray the answer. The other moms will join in one accord, agreement prayer, thanking God with you. Here is an example.

First mom: "Dear Father, thank You that my son has found a Christian friend at school."

Second mom: "Thank You for Your perfect timing. You knew how lonely he was, that he needed a Christian friend to help him be strong in You."

Third mom: "We thank You, Father, for Your goodness and that You truly care about every detail of his life."

When one subject is finished, another mom can introduce the next answer to prayer and so on.

Be sure to dedicate this time to thanksgiving only. It will be tempting to mention requests, but remember to focus on giving thanks.

Intercession—This is a powerful prayer time as we come to God interceding on behalf of children, teachers and staff, school concerns and Moms in Prayer. If your group is large, we suggest you divide into smaller groups of two or three, allowing more time to pray for each child. Each mom chooses one child to pray for each week.

Children. The leader shares a scripture verse to pray for the children. As we pray, placing our child's name in the verse, the power of God's Word drives out anxiety and fear, and produces faith in us. Remember that faith is taking God at His word and acting accordingly. It is accepting God's words no matter what the circumstances or how we feel.

Here is an example of praying in one accord for our children using Colossians 1:10 (NASB), *May _____ (add child's name) walk in a manner worthy of the Lord, pleasing Him in all respects, bearing fruit in every good work and increasing in the knowledge of God.*

First mom: "Dear Father, I ask that David will live a life worthy of the Lord and please You in every way, bearing fruit in every good work, growing in the knowledge of God."

Second mom: "Yes, Father, I ask that David will conduct himself the way a Christian should, no matter how difficult the circumstances."

Third mom: "Dear Lord, I agree with these prayers and ask that David will not live one way at home and church, and another way at school. I ask that his Christian walk would be a part of every aspect of his life."

Second mom: "And Father, that You will open his eyes to what really pleases You, that he will know that obedience brings blessings."

Cover all prayer thoughts from this verse for David before going on to the next child. Pray for each child using this scripture verse before praying a specific request.

After you have prayed scripturally for each child, pray for a specific need of each child, such as salvation, a concern with a teacher, grades, the salvation of friends, choice of friends or communication at home, etc. You may record these requests on the prayer sheet. A blank prayer sheet is at the center of this *Booklet* or go to MomsInPrayer.org for more partially filled-in sheets.

Prayer Suggestions for Our Children

Pray for their relationship with God
- That they may know the unconditional love of God (Ephesians 3:18-19)
- That at an early age they may accept Jesus Christ as their Savior (2 Timothy 3:15)
- That they will allow God to work in their lives to accomplish His purposes for them (Philippians 2:13)
- That they will earnestly seek God and love to go to church (Psalm 63:1; Psalm 122:1)
- That they will be caught when guilty (Numbers 32:23)

Pray for godly attributes
- That they will be protected from attitudes of inferiority or superiority (Genesis 1:27; Philippians 2:3)
- That they will respect authority (1 Peter 2:13-14)
- That they will be the best students they can be (Colossians 3:23)
- That they will hate sin (Psalm 97:10)
- That they will control their tempers (Ephesians 4:26)
- That they will exhibit the fruit of the Spirit in their lives (Galatians 5:22-23)

Pray for relationships with family
- That they will obey their parents in the Lord (Proverbs 1:8; Colossians 3:20)
- That they will accept discipline and profit from it (Proverbs 3:11-12)
- That they will love their siblings and not allow rivalry to hinder lifelong, positive relationships (Ephesians 4:32)

Pray for relationships with friends
- That unsaved friends will come to know Jesus (2 Peter 3:9)
- That they will choose godly friends, who will build them up in the Lord, and be kept from harmful friendships that will lead them astray (Ecclesiastes 4:10; Proverbs 1:10)

MIP prayer sheet

Praise—Praising God for **who He is,** His attributes, His name or His character

Attribute:

Definition:

Scripture(s):

Confession—Silently confessing your sins to the God who forgives

If we confess our sins, He is faithful and righteous to forgive us our sins and to cleanse us from all unrighteousness. 1 John 1:9 (NASB)

Thanksgiving—Thanking God for **what He has done**

In everything give thanks; for this is God's will for you in Christ Jesus. 1 Thessalonians 5:18 (NASB)

Intercession—Coming to God in prayer on behalf of others

Our Own Children—Each mom chooses one child. First pray the scripture then pray a specific request.

Scripture:

2nd Mom's Child specific request:

3rd Mom's Child specific request:

Teachers/Staff—Use the verse below or the verse for your child.

Scripture: Open _____'s eyes and turn him/her from darkness to light and from the power of Satan to God, so that he/she may receive forgiveness of sins and a place among those who are sanctified by faith in Jesus. From Acts 26:18

School Concerns

1. Pray for revival and spiritual awakening at your school.
2. Pray for protection over the staff and students at your school.
3. Pray for other concerns at your school.

Moms in Prayer Concerns

1. Pray that every school worldwide would be covered in prayer.
2. Pray for protection over the ministry, keeping it pure and unified.
3. Pray for more donors to partner with the ministry in equipping groups and reaching the nations.

Remember, what is prayed in the group, stays in the group!

MomsInPrayer.org

- That they will be firm in their convictions and withstand peer pressure (Ephesians 4:14; 1 Corinthians 15:33)
- That they will be friends to the lonely, the discouraged, the lost (Matthew 25:40; Philippians 2:4)

Pray for protection

- From the evil one (John 17:15)
- From drugs, alcohol and tobacco (Proverbs 20:1; 23:31-32)
- From victimization and molestation (Luke 17:1-2)
- From premarital sex (1 Corinthians 6:18-20)
- From physical danger, accidents and illnesses (Philippians 4:6)

Pray for their future

- That they will seek God when choosing a spouse (2 Corinthians 6:14)
- That they will be wise in the choice of a career (Proverbs 3:6)
- That they will use their God-given gifts, talents and abilities for His glory (Matthew 25:21; Ephesians 2:10)

More scriptures to pray for your children

Deuteronomy 10:12-13	Ephesians 1:18-19	Philippians 3:10	2 Timothy 2:15-16
1 Chronicles 28:9	Ephesians 4:1-2	Colossians 1:9-11	James 4:8
Matthew 6:33	Ephesians 4:23-25a	Colossians 2:6-8	1 John 1:8-9
John 17:26	Ephesians 4:29	Colossians 3:1-2	1 John 2:15-16
Romans 12:2	Ephesians 5:1-3	1 Thessalonians 4:3-4, 7	1 John 3:7

Prayer Suggestions for Teachers & Staff

As we pray for teachers and staff, we can be confident that God is hearing and answering our prayers, even though we might not see the results.

Many teachers have shared how much they have appreciated and counted on our prayers. One teacher, with tears in her eyes, expressed that she could not believe we would actually take the time and have the concern to pray for her. She thought the only other person who ever prayed for her was her mom.

Begin by praying a scripture for the teachers/staff

2 Chronicles 19:7	2 Corinthians 9:8	Philippians 1:9-11	1 Timothy 6:20
Psalm 43:3	Ephesians 1:17	Colossians 3:12-15	2 Timothy 2:24-25
Proverbs 2:10-11	Ephesians 3:18-19	Colossians 3:17	Titus 2:7
1 Corinthians 4:2	Ephesians 6:19-20	Colossians 4:3-6	1 Peter 5:2

Specific prayer suggestions for teachers

- That they will accept God's gift of salvation
- That they will teach with excellence and creativity
- That they will use speech that is gracious and pleasant
- That they will consider each child as a special individual, not just as "their class" or "their job"
- That they will have the zeal to make a difference for good in each student's life
- That they will not grow weary in doing good (Galatians 6:9), that their commitment to excellence and discipline will not wane
- That substitute teachers will be able to control classrooms and be a welcome and positive influence
- That teachers going through difficult personal problems will seek God
- That Christian teachers will recognize secular philosophies within the curriculum and openly stand firm in their values

Prayer Suggestions for Schools

As we pray for school concerns, we intercede for God's power to impact our child's school environment.

- That positions at the national, state and local level will be filled by men and women with godly principles and values
- That curriculum will be chosen wisely and that it will include biblical standards and high moral values
- That each student will learn of God's great love and provision for salvation, and accept God's forgiving grace
- That children from difficult family situations will receive godly counsel and compassion from their teachers

- That your school will be drug-free and alcohol-free and no addictions will have hold on the youth
- That God will protect students against unwise choices in extracurricular activities
- That there will be respect for one another, regardless of race or religion
- That every child in the school is prayed for by name, if possible (Yearbooks are helpful for this)
- Pray protection for the school campus

Prayer Suggestions for Moms in Prayer International

As you close your prayer time, take a few minutes to pray for the ministry of Moms in Prayer International. For more specific requests for the ministry visit MomsInPrayer.org.

- For other moms to join your group
- For each school (by name) in your district to have a Moms in Prayer group
- For a group for every school in your city or area
- That every school in your state will have a Moms in Prayer group
- That every nation around the world will have moms praying for their children and schools
- That the Lord will give the Moms in Prayer staff and board of directors wisdom and discernment in all decisions they must make on behalf of this ministry
- That God will keep the ministry pure and untarnished

Praying for the Non-believer

When someone's salvation seems impossible, we need to believe by faith the verse Mark 10:27b (KJV), *With God all things are possible.* We are in a spiritual battle. Thank God that our spiritual weapons are mighty and our authority in Christ is far above the rulers, powers and forces of darkness. The enemy must yield (2 Corinthians 10:3-5). We pray in the name of Jesus, asking for the salvation of students, teachers and staff members. This takes faith, patience and persistence. Remember 2 Corinthians 5:7 (NASB), *For we walk by faith, not by sight.*

Here is an example of one accord prayer for the non-believer using 2 Corinthians 10:3-5:

First mom: "Dear Father, in the name of the Lord Jesus, we pray for the tearing down of all the works of Satan in the life of Sarah."

Second mom: "We pray that her very thoughts will be brought into captivity to the obedience of Christ."

Third mom: "With the authority of the name of the Lord Jesus Christ, we ask for Sarah's deliverance from the power and persuasions of the evil one."

First mom: "We pray that her conscience will be convicted, and that You, God, will bring her to the point of repentance, and that Sarah will listen and believe as she hears or reads the Word of God."

Third mom: "May Your perfect will and purpose be accomplished in and through Sarah."

Suggested scriptures to study and incorporate in your prayer time for non-believers:

Ezekiel 11:19	Romans 10:13-15	2 Timothy 2:25-26
Mark 1:5	2 Corinthians 4:3-4	2 Peter 3:9
John 14:6	1 Timothy 2:4-6	

Promises to Claim

2 Chronicles 7:14 (NKJV)—*If My people who are called by My name will humble themselves, and pray and seek My face, and turn from their wicked ways, then I will hear from heaven, and will forgive their sin and heal their land.*

Psalm 44:5 (NKJV)—*Through You we will push down our enemies; Through Your name we will trample those who rise up against us.*

Psalm 50:15 (NKJV)—*Call upon Me in the day of trouble; I will deliver you, and you shall glorify Me.*

Psalm 84:11 (NASB)—*For the LORD God is a sun and shield; The LORD gives grace and glory; No good thing does He withhold from those who walk uprightly.*

Isaiah 30:19b (NLT)—*He will be gracious if you ask for help. He will surely respond to the sound of your cries.*

Jeremiah 33:3 (NASB)—*Call to Me and I will answer you, and I will tell you great and mighty things, which you do not know.*

Matthew 18:19-20 (NASB)—*Again I say to you, that if two of you agree on earth about anything that they may ask, it shall be done for them by My Father who is in heaven. For where two or three have gathered together in My name, there I am in their midst.*

Matthew 21:22 (AMP)—*And whatever you ask for in prayer, believing, you will receive.*

Luke 1:37 (AMP)—*For with God nothing [is or ever] shall be impossible.*

With God all things are possible.
Mark 10:27b (KJV)

Luke 11:13 (NASB)—*If you then, being evil, know how to give good gifts to your children, how much more will your heavenly Father give the Holy Spirit to those who ask Him?*

John 14:13-14 (NLT)—*You can ask for anything in my name, and I will do it, so that the Son can bring glory to the Father. Yes, ask me for anything in my name, and I will do it!*

John 15:7 (AMP)—*If you remain in Me and My words remain in you [that is, if we are vitally united and My message lives in your heart], ask whatever you wish and it will be done for you..*

John 16:24 (AMP)—*Until now you have not asked [the Father] for anything in My name; but now ask and keep on asking and you will receive, so that your joy may be full and complete.*

Hebrews 10:22-23 (NASB)—*Let us draw near with a sincere heart in full assurance of faith, having our hearts sprinkled clean from an evil conscience and our bodies washed with pure water. Let us hold fast the confession of our hope without wavering, for He who promised is faithful.*

James 1:5-6 (NASB)—*But if any of you lacks wisdom, let him ask of God, who gives to all generously and without reproach, and it will be given to him. But he must ask in faith without any doubting, for the one who doubts is like the surf of the sea, driven and tossed by the wind.*

James 5:16 (NLT)—*Confess your sins to each other and pray for each other so that you may be healed. The earnest prayer of a righteous person has great power and produces wonderful results.*

1 John 3:21-23 (NASB)—*Beloved, if our heart does not condemn us, we have confidence before God; and whatever we ask we receive from Him, because we keep His commandments and do the things that are pleasing in His sight. This is His commandment, that we believe in the name of His Son Jesus Christ, and love one another, just as He commanded us.*

1 John 5:14-15 (NASB)—*This is the confidence which we have before Him, that, if we ask anything according to His will, He hears us. And if we know that He hears us in whatever we ask, we know that we have the requests which we have asked from Him.*

Words and Deeds

While the purpose of Moms in Prayer International is to pray, some groups choose to reach out to the school with written notes, goodies or gifts that we call Words and Deeds. Encouraging and supporting the school staff in this way is an optional activity of Moms in Prayer. Remember, we are not to evangelize by sending gifts or messages with Scripture, Christian slogans, etc. Words and Deeds should never be a burden to the group either financially or in time commitment, and the permission of the principal is required.

It is important for a group to be well established before the leader introduces Moms in Prayer to the principal. A personal visit is recommended. Here are some suggested points to cover:

- Acknowledge your appreciation of the principal's leadership and the tremendous responsibility that he/she has.

- Share your concern for the pressures that young people are facing today.

- Let the principal know that you belong to a group of moms called Moms in Prayer International who meet to support the school through prayer.

- Indicate that your group of moms would like to bring treats at different times throughout the year to encourage and show appreciation to the faculty and staff.

If a principal declines your offer, thank him/her graciously, you can also present a card with your name and phone number, and ask him/her to call you if there ever is a time when the staff might benefit from some encouragement.

Samples of encouragements and additional ideas are available at MomsInPrayer.org.

Statement of Faith

1. **We believe the Bible to be inspired by the Holy Spirit, the only infallible, authoritative Word of God in all matters of faith and conduct.**

   Deuteronomy 4:2; Psalm 19:7-9; Proverbs 30:5-6; 1 Corinthians 2:13; Galatians 1:8-9; 2 Timothy 3:15-17; 2 Peter 1:20-21; Revelation 22:18-19

2. **We believe that there is one God, eternally existent in three persons: Father, Son and Holy Spirit.**

   Genesis 1:1-3; Isaiah 44:6-8; Matthew 28:19-20; Mark 12:29; John 1:1-4; Acts 5:3-4; 2 Corinthians 13:14

3. **We believe in God the Father, an infinite, personal spirit, perfect in holiness, wisdom, power and love. We believe that He concerns Himself mercifully in the affairs of each person, that He hears and answers prayer, and that He saves from sin and death all who come to Him through Jesus Christ.**

   Genesis 21:33; Exodus 33:14; 2 Samuel 24:14; Isaiah 40:28; Jeremiah 31:3, 32:17; John 4:24; Romans 5:8, 11:33-34; Ephesians 1:19-20; 1 John 5:14-15; Revelation 4:8

4. **We believe in God the Son, Jesus Christ the Savior, the only begotten Son of God, in His deity, in His virgin birth, in His sinless life, in His miracles, in His substitutionary and atoning death through His shed blood, in His bodily resurrection, in His ascension to the right hand of the Father, in His continuous intercession for His people, and in His personal return in power and in glory.**

   Matthew 24:30; Mark 8:38; Luke 1:34-35, 24:27; John 1:1-2, 14, 18, 3:16; Romans 3:23-26, 8:34; 1 Corinthians 15:3-4; Hebrews 4:15

5. **We believe in God the Holy Spirit, the Helper and Comforter, in His daily guidance and revelation of truth, in His conviction of sin, righteousness and judgment, and in His indwelling presence at the moment of salvation, enabling believers to live godly lives.**

   John 3:5-8, 14:16-17, 16:13-14; Acts 1:8; 1 Corinthians 12:13; Ephesians 4:30-32, 5:18

6. We believe that everyone is born with a sinful nature, separated from God and in need of salvation. Regeneration by the Holy Spirit is absolutely essential for salvation through the repentance from sin and the acceptance of Jesus Christ as Lord and Savior.

    John 3:5-8, 5:24; Acts 2:21; Ephesians 1:6-7, 2:8-9; Titus 3:5; 1 Peter 1:23

7. We believe in the resurrection of both the saved and the lost; the saved unto the resurrection of eternal life and the lost unto the resurrection of eternal damnation.

    Luke 16:19-26; 2 Corinthians 5:8; Philippians 1:23; 2 Thessalonians 1:7-9; Revelation 20:11-15

8. We believe in the spiritual unity of believers in our Lord Jesus Christ.

    Acts 2:42-47; Romans 15:5-6; 1 Corinthians 12:12-13; Ephesians 4:3-6

"Again I say to you, that if two of you agree on earth about anything that they may ask, it shall be done for them by My Father who is in heaven. For where two or three have gathered together in My name, there I am in their midst."

Matthew 18:19-20 (NASB)

Policies

Each group is responsible to adhere to the policies of Moms in Prayer International. They are NOT optional.

1. Any individual or group not adhering to the Moms in Prayer International Statement of Faith or Policies shall not have the right to use the Moms in Prayer name or logo, nor represent the ministry in any manner.

2. Moms in Prayer International is not a lobbying group, regardless of how worthy the cause. Participation in outside political and social issues must be done solely on an individual basis. Under no circumstances should the Moms in Prayer name be used in conjunction with outside issues.

3. Confidentiality brings integrity to the ministry; therefore, all prayer requests must be held in strictest confidence.

4. Moms in Prayer groups are not to hold their meetings on public school campuses. We pray for the schools, not in the schools.

5. Moms in Prayer groups are not to solicit prayer requests nor place a prayer request box in any public school facility.

6. Moms in Prayer groups are not to use the public schools to solicit membership.

7. Unauthorized use of the Moms in Prayer name or logo is prohibited. It is the trademark of the Moms in Prayer International ministry, and its use requires the express, written permission of Moms in Prayer International.

8. Moms in Prayer rosters are for ministry use only. Under no circumstances are they to be used by, loaned to or shared with any other individual, organization, business or outside group.

9. No form of advertisement may be placed inside or on any Moms in Prayer International materials.

10. To allow for conversational prayer in one accord and to implement the Four Steps of Prayer, during the Moms in Prayer prayer hour we refrain from forms of spirituality practiced and lived in the various denominations, such as speaking in tongues and other possible forms of prayer. This is done out of consideration - without judgment. We respect the unity in diversity, to make it possible for every woman to participate.

11. Moms in Prayer groups are not to engage in gossip or any conversation of a critical nature.

12. Moms in Prayer believes in biblical marriage as the covenant relationship between one man and one woman.

13. Moms in Prayer groups are specifically for women.

*Don't worry about anything; instead,
pray about everything. Tell God what you need,
and thank him for all he has done.
Then you will experience God's peace,
which exceeds anything we can understand.
His peace will guard your hearts and minds
as you live in Christ Jesus.*

Philippians 4:6-7 (NLT)

Core Values & Guiding Principles

The Core Beliefs

We all adhere to the Moms in Prayer International Statement of Faith, a personal acceptance of Jesus into ones life as Savior and Lord, and that Jesus is God.

We believe that through prayer God releases His power on behalf of our children and schools. Our faith is in God who hears and answers our prayers.

The Core Purpose

Mission Statement: Moms in Prayer International impacts children and schools worldwide for Christ by gathering mothers to pray.

Vision Statement: Our vision is that every school in the world would be covered with prayer.

The Core Priorities

- God First
- Family Second
- Ministry Third

The Core Format and Method

- One Accord Praying
- The Four Steps of Prayer
- Praying Scripturally
- Praying Specifically
- Evangelism Praying

The Guiding Principles

We are bond-servants of the Lord, completely dependent upon Him for guidance and help.
We do not trust in chariots or horses, but in the name of the **LORD** *our God.* Psalm 20:7
We are a discipleship and a multiplication ministry.
    Discipleship: teach women how to pray and trust God
    Multiplication: every school prayed for by a group

We have been called to serve in Moms in Prayer.

We are accountable to represent the ministry and vision with love and integrity.

We nurture, encourage and equip with a godly, gracious, uncritical spirit, setting an example of biblical womanhood and sexual purity.

We strongly believe and support God-instituted, biblical marriage as the covenant relationship between one man and one woman.

We have a message that brings encouragement and hope to mothers.

We maintain strict confidentiality - what is prayed for in the group, stays in the group.

We pray for children and schools.

We are **not** a lobbying group: *Moms in Prayer International is not a lobbying group, regardless of how worthy the cause. Participation in outside political and social issues must be done solely on an individual basis. Under no circumstances should the Moms in Prayer International name be used in conjunction with outside issues.*

We will communicate to our financial supporters with the highest professional standards of truth, accuracy, and propriety before God.

> *May he grant your heart's desires and make all your plans succeed. May we shout for joy when we hear of your victory and raise a victory banner in the name of our God. May the Lord answer all your prayers.*
>
> Psalm 20:4-5 (NLT)

Frequently Asked Questions

1. **How do I find another mom to pray with?**

    Go to MomsInPrayer.org to join a group. Also use MomsInPrayer.org to make sure your group is registered so other moms can find you.

    Most people join a group because they were invited by a friend. For this reason, a variety of flyers are available at MomsInPrayer.org. These can be personalized and printed to share with other women at church, in your neighborhood or elsewhere. (Please remember not to publicize your group on a public school campus.)

2. **How do I ensure that my group continues after I leave?**

    We pray that every group will continue until Jesus returns. Please be intentional about training a co-leader or co-leaders who can fill in for you when you or your child are sick or out of town, and who might be willing to pick up the baton of leadership from you if God calls you to another school/group. If you lead a traditional group that prays for one school, be praying for your group's next leader and give the women with younger children an opportunity to lead the group occasionally, so they will be comfortable doing so when your children change schools.

3. **How can I have the most effective prayer time?**

    Pray throughout the week for your group. During the Moms in Prayer hour, use the Four Steps, praying in one accord, agreement prayer.

    A Moms in Prayer group prays for their children and concerns that pertain to their school. Topics other than these must be prayed about before or after the prayer hour.

    Moms with more than one child at the same school are encouraged to focus on one child each week. This allows for more concentrated and specific prayer for that child during the given time for intercession. Moms may alternate children weekly or focus on one child for several weeks or months.

    If a mom has a specific prayer request for the school, she is to give it to the leader before the meeting. This will avoid unnecessary discussion during prayer time as well as give the leader an opportunity to consider if it is appropriate for sharing with the group for prayer.

A mom who knows a teacher personally and is confident that the teacher is a Christian may ask for prayer requests privately. To protect the student's privacy, the teacher should never give the student's name when sharing a personal prayer request.

4. **As a Moms in Prayer mom, how do I handle personal school-related issues?**

   The Moms in Prayer ministry must not be used in addressing any personal issues when dealing with the school. Should a Moms in Prayer mom find it necessary to go to a teacher or principal concerning a child or a school-related matter, she is to go with a gracious spirit as a concerned parent without identifying herself as being part of Moms in Prayer.

5. **What does it mean to be a part of Moms in Prayer International?**

   Moms in Prayer International is a worldwide prayer movement. God is calling moms from Norway to New Zealand, from El Salvador to Ethiopia, to gather in united prayer for their children and schools. The hearts of moms beat the same all over the world.

   For more information about what God is doing in this international ministry, visit MomsinPrayer.org/who-we-are/global-community/.

6. **How can my group support the global ministry of Moms in Prayer International?**

   Your prayers are an important way to support the Moms in Prayer International ministy. See our online prayer calendar at: MomsInPrayer.org/Resources/Prayer-Calendar. You can add a ministry request to your weekly prayer sheet and even copy requests to your Google calendar and share.

   You can also help us share hope and prayer to the nations through your financial gifts. Many groups donate to the ministry so that more women of the world can be mobilized to pray and so that they too can experience the peace and hope that comes with corporate prayer. To give individually or as a group, please visit MomsInPrayer.org/Give or text the word "Partnership" to 91999.

Registration Information

Dear Mom,
Welcome to Moms in Prayer! Please take a moment to register your group or get connected with a group in your area. Simply go to our website and register at **MomsInPrayer.org** OR fill out the form below. If you have any questions or need more information, email us at: **Info@MomsInPrayer.org**

Name _____
Address _____
City _____
State/Province/Postal Code _____
Country _____
Email _____
Home Phone _____
Cell Phone _____

I am a ☐ Group Leader ☐ Potential Leader
☐ Group Member ☐ Not in a group
☐ Other _____

Mail completed registration form to:

Moms in Prayer International
P.O. Box 1120
Poway, CA 92074-1120